THE DEPRESSION BOOK

DEPRESSION AS AN OPPORTUNITY FOR SPIRITUAL GROWTH

EXPANDED AND REVISED EDITION

Books by Cheri Huber and Ashwini Narayanan

The Big Bamboozle: How You Get Conned Out of the Life You Want and What to Do about It

What Universe Are You Creating? Zen and the Art of Recording and Listening

I Don't Want To, I Don't Feel Like It: How Resistance Controls Your Life and What to Do about It

Published by Keep It Simple Books

Books by Cheri Huber

What You Practice Is What You Have: A Guide to Having the Life You Want

There Is Nothing Wrong With You: Going Beyond Self -Hate, Rev. Ed.

The Fear Book: Facing Fear Once and for All

Transform Your Life: A Year of Awareness Practice

The Key and the Name of the Key Is Willingness

Be the Person You Want to Find: Relationship and Self-Discovery

How You Do Anything Is How You Do Everything, Rev. Ed.

Suffering Is Optional: Three Keys to Freedom and Joy

When You're Falling, Dive: Acceptance, Possibility and Freedom

That Which You Are Seeking Is Causing You to Seek

There Is Nothing Wrong With You for Teens

Nothing Happens Next: Responses to Questions about Meditation

Time-Out for Parents: A Guide to Compassionate Parenting, Rev. Ed.

Trying to Be Human: Zen Talks

Sweet Zen: Dharma Talks with Cheri Huber

Good Life: Zen Precepts Retreat with Cheri Huber

The Zen Monastery Cookbook: Stories and Recipes from a Zen Kitchen

There Are No Secrets: Zen Meditation with Cheri Huber (DVD)

Published by Keep It Simple Books

How to Get from Where You Are to Where You Want to Be
Published by Hay House

Unconditional Self-Acceptance: A Do-It-Yourself Course (6 CD set)
Published by Sounds True

Published by Keep It Simple Books
Printed in the United States of America

ISBN 978-0-9915963-6-2

Cover design by Mary Denkinger
sunwheelart@earthlink.net

Eleventh Printing 2019

Table of Contents

Foreword

An essential part of seeing clearly is finding the willingness to examine closely the many ideas and beliefs we hold, almost all of which we learned as children. There are many things in this book that go against what most of us have been conditioned to believe and think. And it takes courage to step into uncharted territory.

If you read something here that seems wrong or doesn't make sense, see if you can slide it onto a back burner, remaining open to whatever truth there is in it. You might see it differently after considering it for a while.

We offer this book neither as an explanation of nor as a cure for depression. Please do not conclude that we are saying you shouldn't seek treatment or counseling. The primary point of this book is to suggest that depression, like anything else in life, can be received as a gift that will aid in your spiritual growth. If you are willing to find compassion for yourself in the midst of the dull pain of depression, you will, perhaps, see how this is so.

In Gassho,
Cheri

So you're depressed...

This book suggests that this is your best opportunity:

to see the cause of your suffering,
to accept where you are,
to embrace yourself in compassion,
to let go and end the suffering.

RIGHT NOW!
not later when you're feeling better.

THREE STEPS
you could take while depressed

1. Pick up this book.

2. Accept the pain and be as kind to yourself as possible.

3. Appreciate yourself for having the willingness to do 1. and 2.

FOR CONSIDERATION:

The state of

DEPRESSION

is not the problem.

The process of

DEPRESSING

is the problem.

If you are depressed, ask yourself,
"What am I depressing?"

When depressed...

you don't want to
<u>deny</u> the experience
nor do you want to
<u>indulge</u> it.

A friend comes to you and says,
  "My husband just left me."
You don't say,
  "Good riddance. He was a toad."
                    AND
you don't say,
  "Here, take these pills. Suicide is best."

SO WHAT DO YOU DO?

EACH TIME YOU ARE DEPRESSED,
stop and turn
your attention inward.

Imagine that you are someone you have no reason to dislike. Pay attention to all your feelings and begin to record them. No analysis, just turn on the recorder and allow your feelings to come out like a volcano. Spew it out. Express it in whatever way. Stay with yourself (this person you like) until you express everything you need to express. Go through all the feelings that arise until it seems like you get to the end of it.

The point?
When you do this kind of process,
you will begin to see patterns.

You will begin to see the steps you take that lead to self-hate and depression. You will notice your fears and assumptions and conditioned reactions to circumstances. It will begin to become clear that depression is something YOU DO, not some larger-than-life ogre to which you are victim.

YOU CAN DO THIS
FOR YOURSELF.

What we're moving toward is letting go of everything that keeps us from
BEING PRESENT WITH OURSELVES.

And the first and last thing
we'll encounter
is fear.

We are afraid of how we feel,
afraid of who we are.

The importance of understanding
depression in general
and yours specifically:

Your depression is not random.

You feel,
   think,
   say,
   and believe the same things every time.

Perhaps <u>what</u> you are depressing changes.
<u>How</u> you depress remains the same.

 The only way we can know
what is going on is to sit down
with an open mind and pay
attention.

If we watch closely enough, we notice that
there are <u>sensations</u> in our bodies that go
with depression.

They don't vary.
They're the same every time.

We have a labeling system that goes with
bodily sensations. In this case, the label is
depression.

With this label comes a learned response,
the internal conversation, everything we've
been taught to believe about depression.

What it is... What it means...
What I am for feeling it...
What will happen as a result...
How the future will be...

When that conversation starts, we have an
emotional reaction to it.
  I don't want this.
  I am afraid.
  This is too painful.
  Oh no, not this again.

And then comes a conditioned _behavior_
pattern, which is usually avoidance/escape.
  I should quit my job.
  I've got to leave town.
  I need a drink (or drug).
  I want a divorce.
  I can't function. (paralysis)
  I'm going to kill myself.

SEQUENCE: sensation
              thought
              emotion
              behavior pattern

THESE ARE GOING ON ALL THE TIME,
not just in depression.

If we are willing
to pay close enough attention,
we notice that in depression:

the sensations in our bodies

don't vary,

the thoughts in our heads

don't vary,

our emotional reactions

don't vary,

our impulses toward certain behaviors

don't vary,

AND THIS CHAIN OF EVENTS
DOES NOT VARY.*

*This is a BIG CLUE.

 Whenever I speak publicly about depression, someone in the audience invariably asks, "What about antidepressant medications? Do you think people shouldn't take them?"

(I think this question is based on a deep belief that spiritual people are here to take away everything that is good, fun, easy and enjoyable.)

My response is something along the lines of: There is no reason to do or not do anything. Whatever you do or do not do,

pay attention.

And then,

to be a bit more encouraging, I might say something like: Do what seems best right now. Do the thing that seems kindest, most caring, most compassionate, and pay very close attention.

Remember, this is a person's life you're dealing with here. The well-being of a being is riding on what you decide.

Should you take this on as stress?
No.

Should you ignore how important this is and go to sleep?
No.

There is an expression in Zen:

"Train as if your hair is on fire."

What does this mean?

It means don't wait. Get immediately into the present moment and do what the moment requires.

If your hair were on fire, it would not be
helpful to panic and race around in all
directions at once...

Nor would it be a good idea to take a nap...

What would be helpful?

Get present, assess the situation, and then move as quickly as possible to the nearest source of help.

And I would encourage you to pull out all the stops. Staying with our hair-on-fire analogy,
dunk your head underwater
grab a fire extinguisher
smother the flames
yell for help.

In other words, if you are depressed,
see your physician
see a therapist
start an awareness practice
learn to meditate.

And my most essential encouragement to you is this:

BECOME AN AUTHORITY ON DEPRESSION

especially your own!

A doctor says something and you find it very interesting. Be open to it but do not accept it on blind faith. Try it. Experiment with it.

A therapist says such-and-such and it may or may not be helpful or true for you. Be open because you are in a no-stones-unturned process, but don't just take it in and take it on because someone with credentials said so.

A spiritual teacher says this or that and your tendency is to agree. But there is no need to agree or disagree — find out! Assume nothing. Look everywhere.

The Buddha said,
"You must work out
your own salvation diligently."

Each of us is solely responsible
for ourselves.

I have a friend from my monastery days who, when given information about herself, responds,

"Thank you. I'll look to see what of that is true for me."

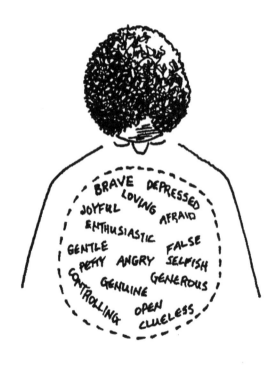

And she does look.

She looks not because she is trying to see what is

WRONG WITH HER.

She looks because

SHE DOES AWARENESS PRACTICE and knows that all insights into her being can lead

away from suffering

and toward freedom.

As you take this approach to depression, your life will begin to change. It will change for many reasons, but I would suggest that the main reason for the change is that

someone is putting interested, kind, caring, supportive time and energy into you and

that's what we want more than anything.

Another question I am frequently asked is, "Can meditation cure depression?"

My answer is YES, ABSOLUTELY, but almost no one is willing to take that route. Why? We want quick fixes. We want to take a pill and never have to face the issues that are resulting in depression.

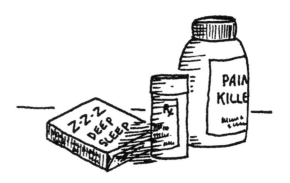

When antibiotics were developed, they were announced with a feeling of finally-we-have-conquered-disease. Today, through gross overuse and misuse, many strains of bacteria have mutated and developed immunity to antibiotics. There is concern among those who study this sort of thing that we are facing a potential crisis.

I have read that experts don't believe the same will happen with antidepressants as has happened with antibiotics, even though there has been, by almost any standards, just as much overuse and misuse.
I lack the belief that the same thing won't happen, and here's why...

If I have bacteria and take antibiotics but don't rest and eat well, the bacteria are probably going to win.

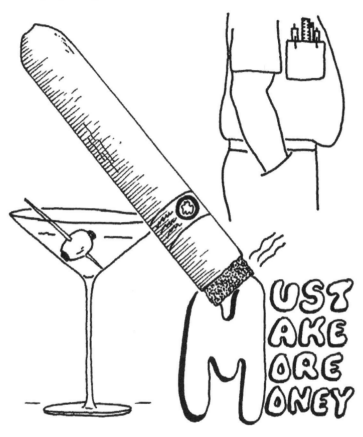

MUST MAKE MORE MONEY

I can take medication for heart disease, but if I don't alter my diet, quit smoking, start exercising and reduce stress, that heart disease is going to do me in.

The person who lives on
    bacon cheeseburgers
    french fries
    soda and beer
will develop some pretty grisly physical
conditions.

Should they be cured by drugs or by a
decent diet?

Is it either/or?

Ultimately, I would wish the person would
realize that that diet kills and quit eating it
altogether
    for the good of the person,
    the good of the cow,
    and the good of the rainforest.

               But that's another story.

We know these things about almost every form of disease that medical science has been able to affect.

Why would it be any different with depression?

Why do we think we can take a pill indefinitely and be cured of depression while we

treat ourselves as if we are indestructible,

ignore signals that we are under too much stress,

take on more than we can handle,

and refuse to give ourselves the same caring time and attention we give to those we love?

When the body is allowed to function
in a balanced
and harmonious way,

it has its best chance to provide
what it needs to be healthy.

As children,
we learned that when we operated from who
we are, we got into trouble.

We learned
        that there is something
                        wrong with us.

We don't want to have that experience again
so we try harder and harder to be the
person we're supposed to be. What we are
suggesting is

THERE NEVER WAS
                ANYTHING
                        WRONG WITH YOU.

It's okay to be who you are,
okay to have all your feelings.
That's what sentient beings have —
                        feelings.

We believe, that if we don't get our hopes up, we won't be disappointed.

"If I'm always disappointed, disappointment won't be so disappointing."

"If I'm not too happy and optimistic, I won't have so far to fall when the bad times hit." The place where most people can recognize that is the times when they've been feeling good for a while and then they start getting nervous that it won't last: This is commonly known as "waiting for the other shoe to drop."

WE
DEPRESS

HAPPINESS

BELIEF: If I maintain a low-grade depression, maybe I can shield myself from real unhappiness.

NOTE: If this page describes you, have you ever asked yourself if this process ACTUALLY WORKS?

Being depressed is like wearing sunglasses with black lenses. When you have them on, everything looks dark.

What color lenses would you assign to other life experiences such as
joy, fear, love, and sadness?

When we respond to circumstances of our lives by putting on the dark glasses of depression and despair, we are responding from lifetimes of conditioning. We have learned that certain situations require certain responses, and the very thought of not responding the way we "should" frightens us, if we even think of it at all.

When we find ourselves wearing those glasses, it is possible, through a process of acceptance and compassion, to take them off.

And even though this notion of ending the depression sounds very appealing, to a part of us it feels like death. It leaves a hole in our identity, an empty space, that usually feels unbearably uncomfortable.

Making peace with emptiness,
becoming friends with spaciousness,
requires great courage.

We are sentient beings
trying not to be sentient, living beings
tensed up against life.

That's depression.

This is what I think.
This is what I feel.
Therefore,
this is who I am,
this is reality.

When we are depressed this seems so
obviously true that questioning it never
occurs to us. And, in a narrow sense, it is
true. It's just that by believing it, we close
ourselves to

universes of possibilities.

Thoughts and feelings are not the same.

EXERCISE

Complete the following:
"How do you feel?"
"I'm depressed."
"That's not a feeling. That's a thought. Look closely. How do you <u>feel</u>?"

A common pattern of confusing thoughts with feelings...

I'm depressed. Something distracts my attention from my misery. For a while I'm not aware of the depression. As soon as the distraction goes away I think, "Oh, I forgot. I'm depressed. I have no reason to be feeling good."

BELIEF: Depression is the only <u>appropriate</u> response to this situation in my life. <u>Anyone</u> would be depressed under these circumstances.

RESULT: The depressing thoughts re-emerge and I'm officially depressed again. "This is real. Anything else is just fooling myself."

Also, we don't need to look for excuses or justification for how we feel.

It is better to just stay focused on how we feel. Then <u>why</u> we feel that way will become apparent.

Trying to figure out
in our head
why we are feeling a certain way
just takes us farther and farther away
from ourselves.

It is never helpful
to use a thought
to figure out a feeling.

For example,

When grieving,
give yourself permission
to feel whatever you feel instead of having
standards about how you should be. It is not
true that certain feelings are okay and
others are not. "Okay" and "not okay" are
thoughts. When we put thoughts in charge of
feelings we get into trouble.
It's not
the feeling we're having that's a problem,
it's our judgement about that feeling.
We could be
feeling anything, and, if we weren't telling
ourselves it was wrong in some way, there
would be no problem. The problem comes
when we reject ourselves for what we're
feeling.

Our feelings are the most intimate experience we have of ourselves. Very often we think we need to blame ourselves for our feelings, or feel guilty about them, and then punish or discipline ourselves.

But really,
what we do about our feelings determines the quality of our relationship with ourselves.

We are responsible <u>to</u> how we feel rather than <u>for</u> how we feel.

If we can create a safe, loving place

within ourselves

for how we feel,
we can create it
for all the aspects of who we are.

Get used to looking
to see how you feel.

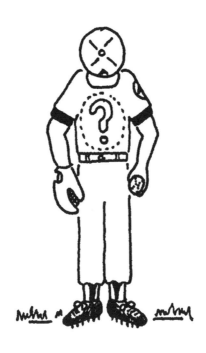

Don't assume you know.

As long as we're depressed, we don't know
how we're feeling. It's only when we say yes
to ourselves and stop depressing that how
we're feeling becomes available to us.

STUDENT AND GUIDE

Student: I would like to explore the relationship between the part of me who gets depressed (I call her The Saboteur) and the part of me who hates her, who is really afraid of depression. The Saboteur says, "What's the use? I might as well give up." If you're like me and have a history of depression doing you in...

Guide — But that's the whole point. It isn't the depression that "does you in." If I wake up one day very depressed and decide, there's just no use in living, that's not a problem in itself. It is my reaction to the depression that can be a problem. This is true in the same way that it would be if you came to me and said, "I'm really depressed. i don't see any use in living," and I said, "You're right. Here's a gun. Shoot yourself." — Do you see? The fact that you're feeling that way isn't a problem. We can guess that

if you came to me and said that, I would say
something to you like, well, what's going on?
how did you get to that conclusion? and you
would start talking about it.

First you would talk about the "whats," the
external elements of your situation. This
isn't working and that isn't working and I feel
this and I feel that. And then we would start
talking about what's under that. Well, this is
going on and that is going on. Then we'd talk
about what is under that. Well... as we
worked down through the layers, we would
get to a place of, I don't like this, I don't
want this, I don't want to be having this
experience.

Well, you are. So, now, how can you sit still
with that? How can you be with that? In our
practice we take the next step of how can
you embrace that. How can you be with that
as though you were with one of your children
who came to you and said, "Mom, I'm

depressed"? You wouldn't say, "Get out of here. I don't want to hear that kind of talk." The work is to develop the same relationship with yourself that you would be willing to have with someone you love. Actually, you would even be willing to have it with someone you hardly know.

Student: Okay, let's talk about the one who is really afraid of hearing that depressed voice inside of me and wants it to go away altogether.

Guide: Because that one is the problem.

Student: Yes.

Guide: This is where we introduce the notion that none of this happens by accident. Because if we simply have the one who is depressed and wants to die, that's manageable. I've been depressed and wanted to die so many times in my life that, you know, I can't take it too seriously at this point.

I say, "Oh, okay. I'm really depressed. So, now, how can I take care of myself while I'm feeling this way?"

And is it fun? No, it isn't fun. And is it going to pass? Probably. It always has before.

There are people who don't even find depression particularly troubling. They have more difficulty with things like happiness or anger. So it's just whatever a person has identified as A Really Big Problem that is one for them.

So there's depression. Big Deal, right? But somebody inside me hates it and is afraid of it. Now, if I get depressed and then get upset that I'm depressed, wouldn't you think that I would want,
                as quickly as possible,

to find out everything I could about depression so that I could manage it or master it in some way?

Student: Well, eventually, yes. I don't think, though that I'd want to do that <u>while</u> depressed... right?

Guide: Well, here's the part of it that's interesting to me. Why is it that if this is a problem and something I want to do something about, why is it that the thing that always arises with it is the very thing that will <u>stop</u> me from doing anything about it? The fear and hatred of it will keep me stuck, not the depression.

Let's say I have a toothache and I really hate going to the dentist, I'm afraid of going to the dentist. I put off going, and the toothache gets worse and worse. But I really don't want to go to the dentist because of my fear and hatred and the pain gets worse and worse and worse. Now, I don't know what would eventually happen. I guess the tooth would fall out or something and the pain would stop. But then what would happen? Another tooth is going to hurt, right? And there are lots of teeth! At some point I would have to admit that by going to the dentist, I might not have this pain. And so, if I remain completely invested in staying with my fear and hatred, wouldn't you become suspicious that there is another payoff for me? Such as: I get to have this miserable experience all the time.

Student: Which is what I'm familiar with.

Guide: Which is what I'm familiar with, yes.

Student: I'd rather do this than change.

Guide: Yes, so I don't think it's an accident that when this depression comes up, right along with it is the reaction that's going to maintain it.

That's one of the things we talk about here at this Center that causes many people to head for the door because it sounds so preposterous. It's just such an absurd notion. "Why would I want to maintain depression? I hate depression. I don't want to be depressed. That's crazy, that's stupid. I'm not doing that. I want to get over this. I don't want to feel this ever again." Well, then, stop hating it.

"How can I stop hating it? If I do that, I'll be depressed all the time. The only thing that's keeping me from being constantly depressed is that I hate depression so much."

No... do you see? The biggest difficulty, as I see it, is to be open to the possibility that what they think is going on just might not be going on.

Everything in our conditioning tells us
that the way to get rid of something
is to hate it,
hate it out of existence,
resist it out of existence.

When we present to a person that
resistance is maintaining the problem, they
tend not to want to talk to us anymore.

OLD ZEN STORY*

Bodhidharma's successor comes to him and cries, "My mind is not pacified. Master, pacify my mind."

Bodhidharma says, "If you bring me that mind, I will pacify it for you."

The successor says, "When I search my mind I cannot find it."

Bodhidarma says, "Then your mind is pacified already."

I'm trying desperately to get rid of something, and I can't get away from it for a second. I drop my resistance to it, invite it in, and it's nowhere to be found. But when I get into a really tight spot, I'm afraid of dropping the resistance.

*Zen Flesh, Zen Bones (1989), Anchor Books

"When you are drowning, you need to relax."

"But how can I relax when I'm drowning? That's nuts! What I have to do is fight for life!"

"No, fighting for life will kill you."

LETTING GO
— a guided imagery —

This imagery is on letting go, and it is, for me, two things. First, it is the disidentification, the movement from being identified with someone or something that is separate. Second, it is the movement back to center, to that openness, the place of acceptance, the experience of being at one with our True Nature, All That Is, Wisdom/Love/Compassion.

In this exercise, I'm going to ask you to relax and go with me as much as you can because what I'm hoping we're going to be able to do is discover, feel, and explore some of the places within us that keep us from letting go.

You can read this guided imagery, pausing at certain points to follow the instructions you are given. Another way is to make a recording and listen to it. You could record it, or you might ask a friend to do it for you.

Begin recording here.

Get as comfortable as you can be, the idea being to stay awake, and start with several long, deep breaths. As you take the breaths, see if you can keep your attention focused on the breath as it
enters your body,
as it fills your body,
and as it leaves your body.

PAUSE (45 seconds to 1 minute; longer if desired)

... just being with the breath, having no concern for anything other than breathing in and breathing out ...

PAUSE

Now as you allow your breath to return to
normal, spend just a moment or so checking
in with your body, allowing your awareness to
expand to include your entire body from
head to toe, being open to the body, aware
of it, sensitive to it in a way that will allow it
to give you any information that it has for
you...

PAUSE

Taking another long, deep breath, shift your
awareness to what you are feeling, to your
emotions... once again being open, being
available...

PAUSE

...see if you can just be open to any insights
your emotions might hold for you today......

Now, another deep breath... and allow your awareness to expand to include your mind — not trying to change anything, improve anything — just noticing.

PAUSE

And now, taking another deep breath, would you just let yourself go... just allow yourself to let go completely and absolutely... Let yourself feel what it is like when you let go completely.

PAUSE

What is this like for you? Is it like laughing, dancing, running? Perhaps as you let go, you are aware that there is something that stops you from letting go completely... So would you allow yourself to become aware of that as completely as you can for right now? What is this that keeps you from letting go? Where is it in your body? What does your body feel like when you're holding on, when you're resisting? What happens with you emotionally when you can't let go? What keeps you from letting go? Is it your emotions? What is it like in your mind when you can't let go? How does your mind keep you from letting go?...... And when you find something within you that keeps you from letting go, see if you can simply acknowledge it. Thank it for taking care of you and protecting you in the way that it does.

PAUSE

...And once again take a nice, deep breath and let go... just feel yourself let go... no restraint, no concern, relaxing completely, absolute faith...

PAUSE

How does this feel? Is it calm? Is it peaceful?... Letting go utterly... See if you can take it to an even deeper level.

If you run into something that stops you, once again see if you can just acknowledge it, just allow it, simply breathing in and breathing out... nothing separating you from All That Is.

PAUSE

Just stay with these things, and when you are ready, bring your attention back into the room and slowly open your eyes.

We hardly ever look at depression because the assumption is so deep that something is wrong with it.
Hide it.
Reject it.
Deny it.

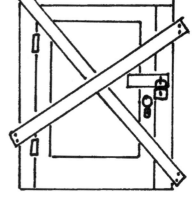

As soon as I see that it's okay, I'm free to explore what it
is.

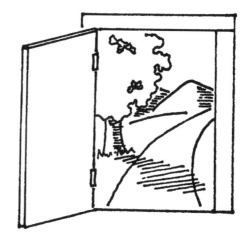

A really good starting point is being open to the possibility that it's nothing like what I have thought it is.

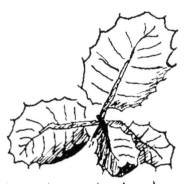

When I was allowed to enter the monastery, my teacher began to help me with a manic-depressive tendency for which I had never sought treatment. He directed me to watch closely how I could go from being very high energy to very depressed and very depressed to very high energy. While high energy, I would have a tremendous sense of well-being, increased creativity, and a fascination with life. At other times, I would feel like I could hardly get out of bed and walk across the room.

One night I was sitting in my room (in the monastery where I trained there wasn't a lot going on) focusing on the energy level in my body. I watched it get higher and higher and higher until it reached a certain point and then I watched it just plummet and collapse in on itself.

What I realized in this experience was that rather than depression being a lack of energy, which I had always thought it was — because when you can't walk across the room the logical conclusion is that you have no energy — it was actually that I had so much my body wasn't able to deal with it.

And even more than that, it wasn't so much that my body couldn't cope as that my conditioned response to myself couldn't cope. I operate within a certain range of vibration or energy or emotion, and when it gets outside of that range it's so uncomfortable my system overloads and circuits start to blow.

Having realized this, two things strike me as very important.

First, I always encourage people to be physically active. We are animals; we are physical creatures. We are designed to move a lot and to work. Exercise helps us "use up" energy and keep our systems balanced. Someone who sits at a desk hour after hour doing stressful or boring work and who has no physical outlet for that energy can go quickly beyond the range tolerance for their system and then go into this depression I'm describing. So I'm always encouraging people to exercise.

Second, the potential problem is that the more you exercise the more stress you are able to cope with. People will tend to exercise, feel better, and then take on more stress and still go to that point of failure or overload where they become depressed.

One of the processes that we pay close attention to in our practice goes like this: there is movement, sensation, a label that goes with that, an emotional response, and then a conditioned behavior pattern (see page 9). As the vibrational level of the body gets higher (sensation), it's sending out signals and they are being interpreted as anxiety or fear or pressure or stress (labels and emotional responses), and then the system begins to try to cope with that (conditioned behavior pattern).

We watch this process closely so that we can begin to let go of the associations we have, the labeling system we have developed to go with the particular sensations. We don't need to change anything. We just need to realize that sensations don't mean anything, and certainly not what we have always thought they mean.

As we understand this process more clearly, as we know that depression isn't something outside our ability to influence, we can make other choices about the level of stress that we are willing to take on, especially when we recognize that building the stress in that way, the energy level getting higher and higher in that way, is one of the first steps in depression.

Guide: In Eastern philosophy there is the concept of chakras. These are energy centers and there are seven of them, ranging from the tip of the spine to the crown of the head. Three of them play a big roll in the relationship between anxiety and depression.

The sixth chakra, located in the head, is where our social conditioning resides. The sixth chakra knows how everything should be and is very concerned with control.

The third chakra, located in the solar plexus, near the stomach (which could explain "butterflies"), is the will center, the center that enables us to exert influence in the world. The third chakra is the "do" center.

The second chakra, located in the belly just below the navel, is the emotional center.

As we are being socialized, we learn to have the sixth chakra (how we have been taught we should be) use the third chakra (the will) to control the second chakra (emotion).

Something very similar to this happens to all of us.

A few years ago a woman told me about her five-year-old being sent home from kindergarten with the message that he was too emotionally immature to attend school — he couldn't control himself. He wanted very much to go to school and understood what he needed to do to be allowed to continue. The woman described how her son would stand, rigid as a board, trembling all over as he tried to control himself.

Taking control,
getting ourselves under control,
controlling our behavior,
(fill in the blank),

are all processes of depressing.

Numbing ourselves with

food
drugs
alcohol
sex
talking
(fill in the blank)

is also a process of depressing.

Student: Yes, what you are saying about chakras and control is how it feels to me. I start to get upset about something and I get nervous. The anxiety builds and the voices in my head are going crazy with all the things that are going to happen if I don't get a grip on myself. My stomach is in a knot... This is where I'm likely to pour myself a good stiff drink.

Guide: Exactly! Anything to numb or dissipate those physical sensations. Many people numb (depress) with food. Others use drugs or sex or talking. This is why I encourage people to exercise regularly as they explore their relationship with anxiety and depression.

Exercise frees energy
blocked in the solar plexus
and dissipates some of it in a healthy way.

However,
meditation will
calm that energy
without deadening,
dissipating or
depressing it.

Student: How?

Guide: As we sit still, attending closely to
exactly what we are experiencing, we realize
that what we have learned to call anxiety
(and learned to be afraid of) is simply
sensation in the body. Energy, the life force
that animates us, moves and we feel the
effects of that movement as sensation.

As we become familiar with the sensation in
the third chakra, we also become more
comfortable with it. As we sit quietly, we see
that those sensations don't mean anything.

At some point in the conditioning process something happened and two things got put together that, in fact, don't go together.

1. That sensation in my stomach...
2. means something is wrong.

As we sit in meditation, watching the sensations come and go, and watching what we label those sensations, and continuing simply to sit, we realize we don't need to cling to that old reaction to a current situation.

Nothing is threatening.
I'm not in any danger.
I'm sitting in meditation.
This is just a sensation in my body.
I don't need to do anything.
If I leave it alone, it will pass.

EXERCISE

Write down what happens with you while you
are depressed.

— I think about this:

— I have these fantasies:

— My heart, stomach, breath do this:

— I stop eating, sleeping, exercising...:

See if you can notice how when you think <u>this</u>
you feel <u>that</u>. Notice how repetitive it is.

How can you know these things?

Sit quietly.
Pay attention.
Believe nothing.

Don't look at something just once. See what is true for you now, and check in again in a week,
in a month,
in three months.

Give yourself a second,
a third,
a fourth chance
to see something anew. Having a new perception and subsequently changing one's mind is not wishy washy.

It is being flexible,
and flexibility is intelligent.

Depression

brings me back to myself
in a way much of life does not.

It gets my attention.
It brings me to a halt.

It says,
"STOP! PAY ATTENTION!"
which I am usually not willing to do
for myself.

DEPRESSION: Life's way of keeping our emotions from happening all at once.

Depression can actually be a way of taking care of ourselves. It can be protection, solace, comfort. We can view it like a soft blanket we can wrap up in.

It's no accident that when people get depressed they often go to bed and eat. We attempt to return to a sort of infant state. We reduce the world to a simple sleep and eat state. Get into a warm place; get tummy full of food. We want to be little and taken care of.

This slows us down and gives us time to find the line between denying ourselves and indulging ourselves. It helps us discover what we really need.

If you are going to be depressed,

BE DEPRESSED...

THROW YOURSELF
A DEPRESSION PARTY

SUGGESTIONS

— Bake yourself a little black cake. Don't put anything in it that would make it rise.

BLACKBERRY

BITTERSWEET CHOCOLATE

— Put on dark clothes, turn on somber music, turn out the lights, get in bed, pull the covers over your head.

— Paint a big, dark depression picture.

What's the point, you ask?

The point is that if you do something like this, you are letting go of your resistance to the depression.

For instance, if you paint or draw a picture of your depression, you have to "get outside of it" in order to form an image of it. In other words, you disidentify from the parts of you who are depressed, and from this disidentified place you are better able to gain some perspective. From this clearer, less painful place you have the opportunity to embrace the parts of you who are suffering.

A little testimonial

One evening a while back I was feeling really depressed. I was having the kinds of thoughts I usually have while depressed: I don't know what I want to do. I don't see any reason to keep trying. Everything is too hard. I don't like where I am but I don't want to be anywhere else, either.

Around and around these thoughts went for a while until I just suddenly said to myself, "Okay, if I am going to be depressed, I might as well enjoy it as much as I can."

I went to the supermarket and bought several of my favorite foods...

Then I went to the video store and rented four videos. When I got home, I moved the television so that I could watch a video and cook at the same time. If I grew tired of one video, I changed it to another. I listened to music I love.

I did anything that I felt like doing.

Self-indulgent? Irresponsible? Absolutely not. The experience was one of spending the evening with someone who loves me unconditionally, who doesn't judge me, who doesn't think it's wrong to pamper myself a little when I'm feeling down.
The truth of the matter
is that it was one of the
best evenings I've ever had.

"How can I know when I'm being self-indulgent and when I'm truly taking care of myself?"

There is, of course, no simple answer to this question. However, here are some thoughts on the matter.

— Self-indulgence is often accompanied by a subtle or not-so-subtle undercurrent of defensiveness or belligerence.
— Taking care of oneself tends to feel like love.
— ODDLY ENOUGH, when we're being self-indulgent, it is rare that we will hear from the voice in our head that asks, "Is this self-indulgent?" It is only when we're taking care of ourselves in a loving way that the voice speaks up.

Why?

Because...

...only egocentricity is concerned with this question,

and egocentricity is
the process of suffering,
of inadequacy,
of self-hate.

So when we are acting out of true compassion for ourselves, egocentricity fights to regain control in ways too numerous and subtle to mention.

We're doing something loving and it says, "Are you sure you're not being self-indulgent?" We're doing something self-indulgent, and it doesn't say a word!

So is egocentricity to be feared and hated? No. Fear and hate are egocentric.

Just don't believe anything it says.

"DEPRESSION"
is a label.
I'm simply feeling the way I feel.

BIG QUESTION:
How much of my problem
is with the way I actually feel,
and how much is with
what I'm telling myself about how I feel?

One of the most commonly depressed
emotions is anger.

When we are children, anger is frightening
because it is so unacceptable to adults.

We feel anger, but
it's more threatening to have it than not to
have it so
we learn to depress it because
we are afraid.

We often turn this anger inward against
ourselves. As adults, we can react with:

-guilt   -illness
-fear   -aggression
-self-hate   -(fill in the blank)

We want to treat emotions
like house guests.

If we give them the
master bedroom with
the hot tub, TV, etc.,
they're never going to
want to leave.

But if we throw a sleeping bag on the floor
of the garage they won't feel welcome.

We want to find the place in between where
they feel welcome but know they're not
invited to stay forever.

Also,

don't meet them at the front door with a shotgun. They'll come down the chimney.

Everyone wants what they can't have. As soon as we make something forbidden, it becomes the most desirable thing in the world. An emotion that feels rejected gets stronger. It becomes like a dog you don't feed enough,

or a child who doesn't get enough attention.

It becomes desperate.

Don't be afraid of your feelings...

Learn to express them <u>to yourself.</u>
It is always safe to express how you feel
to yourself.

Afraid you'll lose control?

You won't. The reason we
lose control is that we
haven't expressed our
feelings.

We think we have to keep our feelings
dammed up or else there will be a flood.

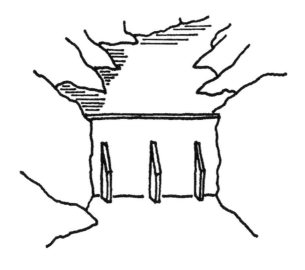

But if we never dammed them up,
a flood would be much less likely!

You can open up to yourself (dare you?) a little at a time until the pressure is down.

All you have to do is acknowledge how you are feeling and then treat yourself as you would treat a friend who was feeling the same way.

"Yes, but:
-I should know better
-I have no right to feel this way
-I've done something very wrong
-I've been treated unfairly
-I brought this on myself
-I yadda, yadda, yadda."

The big question here is "So what?" The most likely reason you're having this experience is that you haven't known how to love yourself unconditionally.

A good beating never helped anything
— except possibly a rug —

and aren't you tired of being one?

Taking that risk often involves learning to trust yourself and

WE DON'T TRUST PEOPLE
WHO BEAT US UP!

If we're going to find out who we are, we have to stop believing the voices in conditioned mind—those hateful voices that beat on us—long enough to get a clear view of who we are.

This is the only way
to find out
who we are.

PRACTICAL SUGGESTIONS
for changing your relationship to depression

SET LIMITS — Say no if life is making more demands than you can meet. Instead of doing and doing until you can't take it anymore and you explode, learn to recognize the signs sooner.

STOP THE BEATINGS — period.

TAKE CARE OF YOURSELF — Do this not in a minimal, miserly sort of way because you feel that's all you deserve, but in a loving, generous way. Be kinder to yourself than you think you should be.

DEVELOP YOUR AWARENESS — Sit quietly. Focus on your breath. Observe your thoughts and feelings, holding on to nothing, pushing nothing away. If you notice yourself tensing up, stop, and return to the breath — no judgements.

Here is a list of "attitudes of mind" more than of "things to do." Read these over and see if any speak to you. If so, start there. Keep in mind that, if you are kind and caring toward this depressed person, nothing you do will turn out wrong.

It might take a lifetime to completely turn this around, but is there anything more important than bringing compassion to the one person you know really needs it? And if that old fear of becoming self-indulgent rises up, just remind yourself that you are in training for being able to be unconditionally compassionate toward all of life. If you cannot be kind to the one person whose suffering you can actually feel, you will never be able to be kind to anyone. This is the most unselfish work a human being can do.

THE LIST

- Consciously put yourself first at least once a day.
- Do something each day just because you enjoy it.
- Break any big task into several small ones. Take baby steps.
- Ask yourself how you feel and listen to the answer.
- Stop assuming you know yourself.
- Be willing to find out one little thing at a time about yourself—baby steps again.
- Lower your standards.
- Rest a while.
- Congratulate yourself each time you accomplish anything!
- Make time for people who make you feel good.
- Say kind things to yourself. Give yourself time off from hard things — no decisions, no big changes.
- Let yourself say, "Me first."

- Practice not believing the negative, critical voices in your head.
- Ask those who love you what they believe about who you are, and then say those things to yourself.
- Go for a walk and take in as much nature as you can.
- Let yourself know you are worth any amount of effort. Find people who can give you support.
- Trust yourself!
- Add your own:

SIGNS... LEADING TO EXPLOSION

✱ I shouldn't be feeling this way. ✱ I have no right to feel this way. ✱ I'm old enough to know better. ✱ I'm just being childish. ✱ It doesn't make sense for me to feel this way. ✱ It's selfish of me to feel this way. ✱ There's something wrong with me for feeling this way. ✱ I don't want to feel this way now. I don't have the strength for this today. I'll deal with this tomorrow when I'm more together. ✱ I don't have time for this today. I've got too much to do to be upset. ✱ I thought I let go of this long ago. Why is it back? What have I been doing wrong? ✱ I refuse to deal with this again. ✱ I'm too tired to do this now, but it's <u>really, really</u> important and I <u>absolutely must</u> get it done right away. ✱ I must exercise self control. ✱ I don't want to do this, but if I don't, her feelings will be hurt. ✱ I have made him dependent on me. I can't stop now. ✱ I have no choice! ✱

☞

...and then later we ask,
"Now, how did _that_ happen?"

Acceptance

The first step is always acceptance. Acceptance precedes even recognition. I will not be willing to see what I'm experiencing until I am willing to accept what I'm experiencing.

As long as we're trying to avoid being who we are or seeing who we are at any level, we are doomed to remain in these conditioned habit patterns that we suffer over.

Each time we grasp our willingness
to see these things,
without judgement if possible,
we take one step closer to freedom.

If you see something about the way you are that you've been taught to dislike and you allow hateful voices in conditioned mind to beat you up for being that way, pretty soon you will be trained to stop seeing.

We don't want to stop looking *regardless* of what we see. We are learning to recognize conditioning and the voices that perpetuate that conditioning. We are learning to have our own present-day experience. Each time we see how we've been conditioned to allow ourselves to be judged and rejected, we want to celebrate the seeing.

Believe it or not, the only thing that gives these negative feelings any power is our fear of them. If you were to welcome them eagerly with open arms, they wouldn't appear. It's really true that the more you genuinely try to invite them, the more unavailable they are.

"All right, I'm ready...."

...I'm going to face this. I'm willing. I'm really going to see how this works...

Okay, come on depression. Come on. Where are you? Talk to me. What have you got to say?"

BIG SILENCE

But the moment I forget and the willingness to be open isn't there,
and I think I've let go of depression,
and I'm hoping I'm better,
and I'm hoping I'll never be depressed again
— the moment I forget not to resist...

IT'S BACK.

Leads toward depression:
-raising your standards until you're dissatisfied
-not doing what gives your life meaning
-repressing how you are and with that depressing the life you know you could be living

Leads away from depression:
-being present
-accepting what is
-not trying to change anything

We tend to believe that if we accept things as they are without trying to change them they'll always be with us. In our experience the opposite is true. We maintain our depression by resisting it. As long as we're resisting, we're putting our energy into whatever it is we don't want.

As soon as we accept the depression, in that moment it is different.

Dear Miserable Person,
your life reflects your
attitude of mind; your
attitude of mind does not
reflect your life. Much love,
your Heart

This is hard information to have, and we are
not suggesting that it's easy to turn this
around.

However,
the fact that we believe it's hard
doesn't mean it's hard.
It just means we think it is.

We can use depression as a tool for self-discovery. We can ask, "What is under this depression?"

We depress what we're experiencing for a reason. For example, I'm angry; I depress that anger, and in focusing on the depression I don't need to see that under the anger is hurt, and under the hurt is disappointment, and under the disappointment is fear.

The boss criticizes me, which makes me angry.
I can't express anger because I'd lose my job.
I'm disappointed because I thought the boss was a friend.
Underneath that, I'm afraid because what I thought was firm is revealed to be shaky.
I'm afraid I'm not going to make it.

Like everything in life
depression can be an ally,.
If we're willing, it has something to teach us.

If I've never been depressed, I can't help
anyone else who is depressed. If I've never
accepted my own depression,
I can't be compassionate
to anyone else's.

How do you begin to uncover what's under the depression?

You GET IT that there's a GOOD REASON* for being depressed and ACCEPT that it's OKAY to feel that way.

Start to EXPLORE what's REALLY going on.

*This GOOD REASON is almost never the one you think it is at first.

We are taught to believe that we have to see something to believe it. As usual, the opposite is nearer the truth.

That is:
I won't SEE what's going on with me because I BELIEVE there's something wrong with it. "I'm depressed. There's something wrong with me."

Or:
I won't SEE that what's going on with me is fear because I BELIEVE that I'm angry and I BELIEVE that anger is wrong.

Just for a little while
be open to the possibility that

there is nothing
wrong with you.

CENTERING
A Guided Imagery

This exercise will assist you in two primary ways. First, you will experience yourself slowing down. This makes it easier to focus your attention. Second, you will experience "center," defined here as your core of wisdom, love, and compassion, your inherent goodness.

--If recording, start here.--
Get as comfortable as you can, close your eyes, and take several deep breaths. Feel the air as it enters your body, fills your body, and leaves your body.

PAUSE

Now shift your awareness to your body... can you feel the outline of your body as it rests against whatever you are resting on?

If you feel discomfort in some part of your body, and, if you need to move to release it, do so...

Now, shift your awareness to your feelings... what are your feeling right now?... calm, anxiety, anger, joy?... Where are you feeling this feeling?... What would be the opposite of this feeling? Can you be aware of yourself going to that opposite feeling in order to recognize and know it?... Where in your body do you feel this opposite feeling?

PAUSE

And now, shift your awareness to your mind... How are you able to see your mind?... Who is it that is able to see your mind? Just observe the activity that is going on in your mind right now...

PAUSE

Now focus on the word <u>center</u> and on the concept <u>center</u>... and now on the experience of center...... Has your attention shifted to that place or feeling that is your center?... If not, focus there now and just experience your center as fully as possible...... Can you become aware of the energy, the vitality, the life that is your center?... See if you can feel that...

PAUSE

And now, let that energy begin to grow, to expand and move through your body. Feel it in your back, in your shoulders, your abdomen, your chest, upper arms, forearms and hands... Can you feel this energy in your legs, your feet... how about in your toes?... Can you feel it in your neck, your scalp, your face?...... See if you can feel this energy throughout your entire body all at once.

PAUSE

Are you shifting your attention from place to place in your body to experience this feeling?... or have you moved back from yourself in order to feel it everywhere at once?... Look to see how you are experiencing this feeling...

PAUSE

Continue to focus on this life force, this vitality throughout your body... Where do you feel it most strongly?... Do you know how you are able to experience this feeling?... See if you can increase the feeling, intensify the sensation...

Stay with this experience for as long as you like, and when you are ready, bring your attention back into the room, and slowly open your eyes.

This moment is the only moment you have.
HAVE IT!
Don't be afraid
to experience your experience.

There is nothing to fear.
There is nothing in the universe
that wants you to suffer.

Rather than focusing on what you want
to have... or get... or do,
focus on how you are — NOW —
because how you are now
is all you'll ever experience.

Projecting into the future from a present depression causes me to see a depressing future...

I believe that what I'm experiencing is real. If I let go of that and get into the present, I realize the present is quite manageable. Nothing awful is going on except the way I feel, and if I didn't hate the feeling, it wouldn't be awful.

Coming back to the present allows me to focus on what is really going on instead of overwhelming myself with imaginings.

The feeling is only a feeling; the label is upsetting.

How I treat myself
in depression
is more important than getting over it
or what I'll do when it's over.

Hating and rejecting myself
in this moment
is not good practice
for loving and accepting myself
in another.

When I stop depressing the feelings, I can begin to take care of the parts of me who feel isolated,
vulnerable,
and afraid.

If I stay in the depression, I'll never see what is underneath it.

We don't need to be afraid of our feelings because of how we think they're going to make us act.

Life keeps saying...

and we keep saying...

Life keeps giving us opportunities to take responsibility and end our suffering, and we keep turning them down!

Some practices say many are called but few are chosen. This practice says everyone is called, almost no one answers.

Student: Will you define what you mean by taking responsibility?

Guide: Yes, I am referring to starting out, right now, to respond to what is. In this evening's context, it has to do with depression and our relationship to it. However, it can be our relationship to anything.

I've chosen depression because so many people struggle with it. It tends to be something that people think is an obvious block to spiritual practice. A person who is acutely depressed will feel they have to get over the depression before they can do spiritual practice. I'm putting forth the notion that spiritual practice can be done with depression, that it is a wonderful thing to work with. So are grief and loss and illness. Anything can be a wonderful thing to work with.

If I'm committed to a spiritual practice, and one day I find myself depressed, I can begin to focus on how I do this process of depressing. I can notice that I have always responded to depression in certain ways, and I can decide to respond to it in a different way.

What will that be like?

The way I think about this is that I am going to become the person who is going to help me with this. I'm going along in life never having felt strong or supported and, suddenly, someone comes into my life who wants to help, who wants to give me support, who wants to listen and talk and explore things with me. On top of that, this is someone who loves me unconditionally and wants to be with me <u>all</u> <u>the</u> <u>time</u>!

This person never criticizes me or tries to change me or thinks I should be different.

ISN'T THAT A DREAM COME TRUE!

It would be wonderful if heaven would open up and drop someone like that into my life,

but have you ever noticed
how seldom that happens?

So I realize that I can be that person for myself. I can come back to a centered place, move into unconditional love and acceptance and have the same attitude toward myself that I have toward anyone else I love.

We can let go and be free
in a moment.

But will we?
Probably not.

But that just means we won't;
it doesn't mean we can't.

The difference between allowing yourself to feel real pain or depressing that pain

is the difference between being cut by a knife or enveloped by fog.

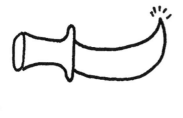 

The cut will heal, usually quicker than you think, and life can go on. But you can live your whole life in the fog, buffered against the experience of pain.

The sadness is that
when protected from pain
we are also protected from joy.

Being depressed and unhappy sometimes is just part of life.

It doesn't mean that something has gone wrong with life any more than rain is something that has gone wrong with the weather...

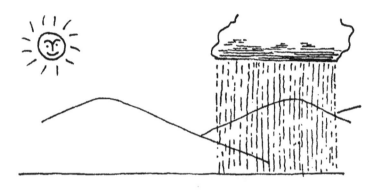

or night is something that has gone wrong with day.

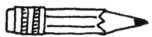

WHAT KIND OF PERSON DO I WANT TO BE?

WHAT KIND OF RELATIONSHIP DO I WANT WITH MYSELF?

HOW WOULD I LIKE TO TAKE CARE OF MYSELF?

WHAT DO I DO INSTEAD?

EXERCISE

Put a check mark next to the things you would say to your best friend if he/she were depressed and came to you for help.

--You shouldn't feel this way. It's a sign of weakness.

--Would a big hug from someone who loves you help?

--Are you being kind and gentle with yourself?

--Just stop feeling that way. It's all your fault anyway. You asked for it.

--You're probably going to be depressed forever.

--Can you just let yourself be depressed without hating it?

--I don't want to be around you when you're depressed.

Now, go back over the list and put a check mark next to the things you say to yourself when you are depressed.

Everyone has one person to take care of.

Be sure you take care of you <u>before</u> you try to take care of someone else.

AGAIN:
Learn to say YES to you <u>before</u> saying YES to others.

AND AGAIN:
Take care of your needs <u>before</u> attempting to take care of another's.

This won't make you more selfish.
It will make you more generous.

We want to try to take care of others
instead of ourselves
because
we can't take care of anyone else
and we can take care of ourselves!

What we are suggesting is that not taking
care of ourselves is designed to perpetuate
suffering.

Why would we want to perpetuate suffering?

- It's familiar.
- It's what I think I deserve.
- It's safe.
- It's what everyone else does.
- I don't have to take responsibility.

How do you feel about having pleasure?
Explore your beliefs.

If self-denial made you a better
person, wouldn't you be one by now?

Living your life in fear that you're going to do it wrong

is like an explorer who is afraid of getting lost...

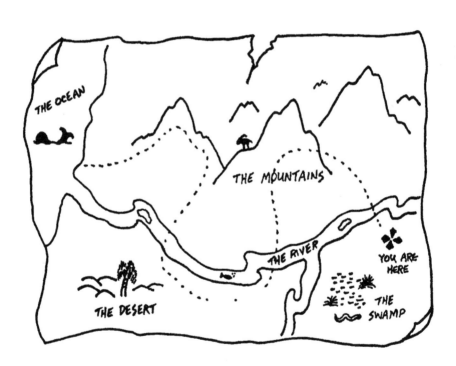

We are conditioned from childhood. Growing up is a process of having one's autonomy removed in order to be socially acceptable, compliant. And generally speaking, the better you learn that, the worse off you are.

Finding yourself,
following your heart,
doesn't mean you will become
socially unacceptable.

Think about heroes, pioneers, geniuses, inspirational people — they are focused on that which gives their life meaning, not on being socially acceptable.

First is commitment to being true to themselves; second, maybe, to what the world expects.

Projection

It is good to recognize that the expectations of others, the standards they expect us to meet, are really our own projections. We judge ourselves by our standards, project them out onto other people, then believe that they think those things about us.

A POSSIBLE SCENARIO
I'm depressed; I hate being depressed; I'm judging myself for being depressed. I look at my friends; I think they hate it when I'm depressed; I think they are judging me.

IN FACT
They may have no reaction to it at all. They may not even notice. It's my standards that aren't being met!

YES, BUT
What if they tell me they hate my depression?

If your friends tell you they hate your depression, you can know that's their problem, just as it would be your problem if you hated theirs.

We hate and avoid in others what we're not willing to face in ourselves.

The ways I think the world expects me to be are the ways I've been taught to believe I should be.

People are judging and criticizing and dismissing me all the time, but as long as I'm meeting my standards of how I should be, I don't even notice.

As soon as I don't meet my standards, I think other people know that I'm not and are judging me as harshly as I'm judging myself.

Are you willing
to give up your life
for what you think
other people
might be thinking?

Think about it.

Has giving up your own life
brought the acceptance and approval
you've always wanted?

Has not being who you really are
brought the joy and fulfillment
you've been seeking?

We deny ourselves our life, close our options because we think society expects us to, we think people will judge us, we think it's too selfish to do otherwise. We take the path that seems safest.

Then, because we're depressing our passion, our desire for life, we eventually move into despair and ask ourselves, Why go on?

A valid question.

We end up with just the hard stuff,
the shoulds,
the have to's,
the things we were trying to avoid in the first place.
We end up with emptiness
exhaustion
meaninglessness. ⇨

The good news is
    none of what society or culture
    tried to get you to believe
    was true in the first place.

There never have been any limits. There
never was anything wrong with you,

                        and there still isn't.

You can be whatever you choose, and the
proof of that is that you are now.

When I'm feeling good,
I'm a good person.
When I'm feeling bad,
I'm a bad person.

If I'm happy I'm right, I'm good.
If I'm not, I'm wrong, I'm bad.

The choice of words in our language shows
the priority "good" and "happy" have.

Depression can happen when we try not to
be unhappy.

We want to go from one peak to the next

without traveling through the valleys below.

peaks/valleys   up/down   right/wrong
One cannot exist without the other.

If what we think is wrong with us were really wrong with us, we would have been able to fix it by now.

The fact that we haven't been able to fix it is proof that it's not really the problem.

The problem is that we have been taught to believe there's a problem. it's like being told that something is broken and trying and trying to fix it and never succeeding.

Because it isn't broken.

There is no problem.
Stop creating one.

Feeling guilty over being how you are
does nothing
but rob you of your life.

It is okay to
feel whatever you feel
think whatever you think
be however you are.

Guilt and fear keep us from knowing our
True Self, our intrinsic purity and goodness,
the Divine within us.

Whatever you are doing, love yourself for
doing it. Whatever you are thinking, love
yourself for thinking it.

If you don't like it,
love yourself for not liking it.

Can you be open to the possibility that if you were who you really are

you would have the approval and acceptance you've always wanted? From yourself if from no one else?

The only approval we really care about is our own.

If I feel I've done a good job, I feel good. If not, I don't.

It doesn't actually matter to us what others think.

PROJECTION, AGAIN

Here's how it works in part:

LOOP:
I won't be who I am because I'm afraid others won't approve. I try to be who I "should" be and I don't approve. I don't approve of me. I project that disapproval onto others and then believe they disapprove of me. I feel disapproved of!

Therefore, it seems I have proof there's something wrong with me.

And there kind of is.
                    I'm caught in this awful loop
                              of my own making.

IRONY:

We endlessly seek other people's approval
when the only approval
that means anything to us

is our own.

If I'm living the life
I want to live,
it's clear
that nobody owes me anything,
and from that place of being satisfied,

I can be much more generous.

Whatever you do, recognize that you are
doing it for you and enjoy it.

If you realize you no longer want to do it,
STOP.

"Isn't that irresponsible?"
You'll never know until you stop and find out.
You could practice with some of the many
little things you do and hate but continue to
do because you believe you should or
someone told you you should.

If you're responsible
because you're afraid not to be,
you're not responsible,
you're afraid.

We all know things we stopped doing when we started growing up. Here are some we came up with. Can you add your own?

playing in the woods
lying on back watching clouds
knowing God
skating
playing baseball
drawing and painting
singing
getting excited about holidays
reading a book over and over
scribbling
playing in puddles

We have to face eventually that we don't want to be undepressed. Terrible things might happen to us if we're not depressed!

We have our identity in this process of depressing. We are afraid that if we stop, we won't know how to be,
won't know who to be,
won't know what life will expect.

It is safer and more comfortable to continue with the depressing than to risk the freedom.

Is this depressing?

Can I realize I do this (reject well-being)
without being depressed about it?

It's depressing to realize
that I've spent my whole life
depressing myself.

The most depressing part is that I've
thought it was external. Now I'm getting the
sense that it is something I've learned to do
and now do to myself.

To say this is depressing information is like
saying that you are on a sinking ship and you
have just discovered a lifeboat...

You can stand there and be upset that the ship is sinking,

or you can take the lifeboat.

The lifeboat is the information in this book.

Take it and go.

Don't waste any time.

The perspective of this book
is that there is nothing more important
than compassion.

The compassion we're talking about might
not look nice and polite. It doesn't
necessarily mean doing what others want you
to do or being how they want you to be.

We're talking about
being compassionate with yourself
because everything else springs from that.

IT IS NOT SELFISH TO LOVE YOURSELF.

And if you can't find compassion for
yourself, you'll never find it for anyone else.
You won't know how. You will never be truly
generous to anyone else while depriving
yourself.

The reason we don't tell anyone they <u>should</u> follow the suggestions in this book is that a person <u>won't</u> until they're ready.

Most people never will be ready, in this life.

All we're saying is that when you're ready here's the way you can stop being victimized by the sensations and voices and reactions of depression.

This is definitely not another stick for you to be beaten with.

When you've suffered enough,
you'll remember that you know
how not to suffer.

It doesn't really matter what you have thought, believed, felt or done before.

This is a new day.

"But I've always done it this way."
"But I've always been this way."
"This is just how I am."

These are three of the world's WORST EXCUSES.

Let's sum up:

Get to know your emotions and learn to have them in healthy ways. Learn to express the energy of emotion in ways that take care of you and those around you. No guilt or blame!

Rest, eat well, exercise regularly, and prove to yourself that tension does not lead to control.

Take up an awareness practice that enables you to let go of beliefs and assumptions about how you and the world should be. This will enable you to live in the current moment, which soothes body,
                    mind,
                        spirit,
                            and emotion.

It is okay to change.
It is okay to try something new.
It is okay to try something rather radically
new, such as the approach we are offering in
this book. (There isn't really anything new
about it. It's just new to many people in our
culture.)

Because if you try it and don't like it, you
can always return to how you were doing it
before. No problem. No shoulds. Trying
something once or twice doesn't mean you
ever have to do it again if you don't want to.

And not taking a risk because you are afraid
is a grave disservice to yourself. Fear is not
the problem. You can have your fear and
allow it to stop you, or you can have your
fear and risk anyway. Either way, the fear is
there. The choice is yours.

Afterword
The Essence of
Recording and Listening Practice

Since this book was written, Recording and Listening has become one of our primary practice tools. I make the point regularly that it is not possible to be depressed with a recording and listening practice (R/L for short). By R/L practice I don't mean picking up a recorder and talking once in a while or listening when the voices in conditioned mind aren't telling you not to. I mean a dedicated practice of using the recorder to have your attention on something other than the conversation in conditioned mind.

That conversation, what we call "ego" (short for egocentric karmic conditioning/self-hate), the illusion of being a "self," a "someone" that is separate from Life, is a system. That conversation is devoted to suffering. If you want to, if it's easier, think of it as all the negativity that goes around inside your head. If you've ever tried to stop it, you know it is not something over which you have control. If you attempt to stop it, it will tell you that the reason you can't is that there's something wrong with you, there's a lack or flaw in you. You're to blame for it. You are doing it. If you really wanted to stop it, if you were a better person, you would stop it.

None of that is true, and we can stop it! The first step is realizing that "I" am not "it," and "it" is not "me." That conversation is not something I'm doing. What is aware of this phenomenon, what is able to observe this process, is not the egoic process, regardless of what the voice in the head claims. That ego illusion, the appearance of being a "separate self," is created and maintained through that incessant brainwashing conversation inside the head.

 Recording what is going on for us and listening to it helps us see that the "conversation in conditioned mind" is not "me."

Learning to step back and observe the conversation shows us that what we are is the *awareness* that can observe it. Quickly we can see that it just goes on in an endless loop. We watch it happen and we realize that we are able to see it and hear it, but we are not *doing* it. When we realize this, we realize what it is and what its "purpose" is in our lives, which is to keep us in the artificial "reality" of suffering that it is creating. It does this to keep itself, the illusion of being separate from Life, at the center of attention—and ego feeds on attention!

 Recordings help us remember "I am not the author of my depression. The negative conversation is."

Once you see that what you're reacting to, what is *depressing you*, is a constant drone of what's wrong—what's wrong with you, what's wrong with others, what's wrong with the world, how bad things are, how difficult everything is, stories about mistakes in the past, an unhappy future, comparisons with other people who have it better, who are better—you begin to see the "source" of your depression. If anyone spent every moment of every day watching and listening to upsetting, painful, distressing, grim, gloomy, and sad movies, we would hardly expect that person to be upbeat and cheery!

 We can make recordings that remind us that we don't have to live immersed in or listening to painful, distressing, and gloomy voices.

To free ourselves from this predictable result of a conditioned process—be subjected to depressing information/feel depressed—we must learn to direct attention *away* from that depressing onslaught.

We can make recordings about what we love, what we are grateful for, what we appreciate, what gives us joy. This allows us to have attention on something other than the negativity of the voices.

It is important to realize that we are not turning attention to the way we've been told our life should be or how we'd like our life to be or wish it were or know it could be if we were just disciplined enough to improve ourselves enough to be the people we are supposed to be. None of that.

That process is how we got depressed in the first place and it's how we stay depressed!

It is possible to turn attention away from it and bring attention *here* to this moment, to the present, to what actually is. Now, what is that? That (THIS) is Life unfolding and as we are present to it we quickly see that Life unfolding is a conscious, compassionate process. Recording and Listening assists us to tune in to the wisdom, love and compassion that is Life unfolding.

 What would wisdom have to say to the knottiest problems that we are presented with? What message of appreciation would be received from that which loves us unconditionally? What encouragement (solace?) would compassion offer when we are tired, aching, disappointed, unhappy, hurting, upset?

Finding the "Mentor," an "embodiment" of the wisdom, love, and compassion that is our authentic nature, gives us moment-by-moment access to the support we need. Instead of living in a conversation that is negative, self-hating, and depressing, with an R/L practice we can live in a conversation of kindness, compassion, and encouragement.

In Gassho,
Cheri

Talking Your Way

through Depression

A Recording and Listening Practice
Self-Guided Retreat

Recording and Listening Practice:
A Brief Overview

To begin:
Obtain a recording device. This can be a handheld digital voice recorder, an app for your smart phone, or an older technology. Recording software on a laptop will get you started, but it's best to have something you can carry around.

To jump start your R/L practice:
Make a recording of everything you love, are grateful for, find beautiful and kind and generous and touches your heart. If you choose, record favorite quotes and music. Add what you value in your life, what you want to attend to, what takes care of you, how you want to feel, etc. Make your first recording while looking at your favorite tree, animal, or view of nature. Listen to your recording three times.

Here is what I have noticed:
We fall in love with our recordings. We find we prefer being in a conversation of lovingkindness and compassion about ourselves and our lives instead of being beaten up by self-hating voices.
Listening to recordings is an act of receiving the unconditional love and acceptance that frees and heals us.

For much more information on R/L practice, go to www.recordingandlistening.org.

ENCOURAGEMENT & SUGGESTION

ENCOURAGEMENT
Being gentle with yourself is the prerequisite for beginning your exploration of how the process of depression/depressing works.

It's not necessary to be a victim of depression. How depression happens can be scrutinized, understood, and transcended. Shining the light of conscious compassionate awareness into its darkest corners can free us of depression's tyranny.

SUGGESTION
Each time you are depressed, do these exercises. On your recorder create a folder for each particular episode of depression. Title it, date it, and then record and listen to your answers. If it feels overwhelming to answer all of these questions, just pick one. Remember, all we're doing is bringing awareness to a process called "depression."

You can do this!

Even if the voices of depression are insisting that you can't,

DON'T BELIEVE THEM. MAKE YOUR RECORDINGS ANYWAY.

And NOW, with recorder, kindness, courage, and resolve, begin your retreat...

Exercise One

Sit quietly for a moment and allow yourself to return to the time you decided to read this book.

Why did you pick up this book?
What drew you to it?
What did you hope it might do for you?

Now record and listen to your answers.

Exercise Two

To make peace with depression we must first face it. With conscious awareness we must confront head-on all aspects of the process labeled "depression."

1. When you consider that, are you aware of any resistance? Are you aware of any fear?

2. To get past your depression, what are you willing to consider? (Example: I am willing to consider that depression is a conversation in my head that repeats endlessly and takes me down the same dead end every time. And I'm willing to consider that that's a BIG CLUE to what's really going on. And I am willing to go up against that conversation and use my recorder to get past it.)

Now record your answers and listen to them.

Exercise Three

Do you know what is being depressed?

We often think of depression as something that *happens* to us. In this exploration we're going to see, without judgment, blame, or self-hate, that depression is something that is *done*, something we *allow*.

Take a little time to sit quietly and see what arises in response to the question, "What is being depressed?" Notice any voices that talk to you about this. Those voices are a big part of the depression process and you'll see/hear them more as we proceed.

Record and listen to what you see about this.

You can't do this wrong. There are no right or wrong answers. We are practicing awareness, paying attention, noticing, getting clearer as we go along. Over time, you might do these exercises many times and each time see more and see more clearly. We're just getting started!

Exercise Four

What do you say when you are depressed?

Recall previous times of depression and see if you can remember what you say as a depression is coming on, as it takes over, as you're in the middle of it, and as it passes. What do you say to yourself? What do you say to people close to you? What do you hear "inside your head"?

Example: I have heard things along the lines of "I'm not feeling well" and "Oh no, not again, I can't do this again," which are both excuses for withdrawing from the world. I've heard "You need to get a grip. What's the matter with you? Get it together!" This is an attempt to force myself to show up and keep going.

What you hear might be quite different.

These are subtle distinctions so take the time you need to get a sense of what is so for you.

If it helps, write these things down before making your recording.

What I hear:

Now record and listen to your answers.

Exercise Five

How do you feel when you are depressed?

Circle one or more of ours, and/or draw your own here.

Record and listen to your answers.

PLEASE CONSIDER...

On pages 8, 9, and 10 you were introduced to some crucial information that I'd like to expand on. To review, this sequence goes on inside of us all the time:

1. sensation
2. thought
3. emotion
4. behavior pattern

It takes a fair amount of paying attention, of watching closely, to recognize that sensations (1) in the body are only sensations, and that they don't have any inherent meaning. "Depression" is a thought (2), a label, a word that has been attached to particular sensations. The thought of depression evokes emotions (3)—dread, despair, etc.—which are followed by conditioned behaviors (4)—indulge old habits, overeat, etc.

Learning to direct attention
to actual sensations—
rather than
labels, stories,
beliefs, and assumptions—
dramatically reduces
the conditioned voices' ability
to drag us into fear,
dread, anxiety, worry,
guilt, and regret.

Exercise Six

Remember, sensations don't mean anything that we haven't decided they mean.

Describe the sensations in your body when you are depressed. (This is one of those very tricky places given that we have a lot of confusing and erroneous information about sensations/feelings/emotions.)

TIGHT SHOULDERS   NERVOUS STOMACH
WRINKLED BROW
HEAVY HEAD   TINGLING HANDS

What are you believing the sensations mean?
Now record and listen to your answers.

Exercise Seven

How do you behave when you are depressed?

We take a GIANT leap toward freedom when we learn that just because we're feeling a particular way and having particular thoughts, we don't need to behave in a particular way.

Example: The thought "I don't feel like it" is rarely recognized as simply a thought that has been triggered by sensations in the body.

(We usually think the thought came first, but it didn't!)

We believe we really "don't feel like it" and we don't do it. Or we do it but are unhappy about it. Until we look at the thought "I don't feel like it" with conscious compassionate awareness, we don't recognize it as the conditioned reaction it is.

Similarly, it is not necessary for the thought "I am depressed" to dictate particular behaviors. Granted, it can be difficult not to be led down those old, well-trodden roads, and we most often are. But with your recorder, kindness, courage, and resolve, you can break that cycle.

So again, how do you behave when depressed?

Now record and listen to your answer.

Exercise Eight

Let's look at stress and depression.
Do you ignore signals that you are stressed?

Do you know how you *feel* when you're stressed? What are the sensations in your body? What kinds of thoughts go through your mind? What kinds of things do you say to people? Are you aware of the conversation that drives you? What are you told that makes you believe being driven beyond your ability to be in sync with the pace of Life is worthwhile?

Now record and listen to what you see about this.

Exercise Nine

An Emotions Check-Up

satisfaction   worry   anger

joy   sadness

envy   fear   resentment   bravery

impatience   eagerness

disappointment   hatred   exhaustion

rejection   excitement

happiness   jealousy

irritability   enthusiasm

(add your own)

What emotions are you not allowed to have?

 R/L about emotions you are not allowed to have.

What emotions are actively rejected?

R/L about which emotions are rejected.

What emotions are indulged?

R/L about which emotions are indulged.

Exercise Ten

This is very important: Getting in touch with the truth about how we feel, what we've been conditioned to believe about how we feel, and our relationship with how we feel is facilitated by expressing how we feel.

There are many ways to express feelings. We can "make them visible" through drawing, painting, writing, or something similar. We can talk with a friend or a counselor. We can do yoga or dance or participate in sporting activities. And, our particular favorite, we can talk into a recording device. Each one of these, if we are to receive benefit, requires us to *pay attention* as we engage in them.

Example: As a person given to rage, I hit baseballs and ran up hills to move the energy in my body out of stuck patterns I'd believed were real. As I ran up a hill, my breathing labored, my heart pounding, the stories in my head would get angrier and angrier.

The sensations of exertion were the same as the rage sensations, but I wasn't mad at anyone as I toiled up those hills!

The sensations had become attached to angry stories. Every time I felt those sensations I would get a download of rage-filled images and memories.

Eventually the stories created the sensations and the sensations fueled the stories.

Realizing that, I could begin to tease apart the components. Soon I could feel the sensations and not go into a rage. I could feel the energy rise up, stay present with it, not get pulled into old stories, and simply have the energy for myself to use as I chose—maybe dance!

What are your beliefs about will happen if you express your feelings? How are you stopped from expressing them?

 Record and listen.

Exercise Eleven

How does the world look when you are
wearing the lenses of depression? Draw the
world!

As you watch the process of depressing,
does the world or life or you
look a particular way, or are
you told the world, life, or you
are a particular way?

Record and listen.

Exercise Twelve

What processes of depressing do you engage with?

Do you attempt to distract yourself from how you feel? If so, how do you distract yourself?

Do you attempt to control how you feel? If so, how do you do that?

 Record and listen.

Exercise Thirteen

Self-hate
is the root cause
of depression.

What are you told is wrong with you?
What about you is judged as unacceptable?
How are you judged for being depressed?

That was a dumb thing to do!

Won't you ever learn?

You shouldn't feel like this.

You should know better!

Record and listen to what you've seen.

Exercise Fourteen

Two-Handed Recording

Recording and Listening practice offers ways to embrace all that arises in life in conscious compassionate awareness.

Two-handed recording is the practice tool recommended when the "going gets rough."

Here are the mechanics.

Step One

Place the recorder in your right hand and start recording. Talk to the recorder as you would a close friend or a therapist. Really allow yourself to express what you are feeling, without censoring. Say everything you ever wanted about what you are going through.

Step Two
Stop the recorder. Breathe. Sit with this experience.

Step Three
Then, placing the recorder in your left hand, listen to the recording you just made, giving it your full attention. Really listen.

Step Four
Keeping the recorder in the left hand switch it on and offer what comes up for you to assist and comfort the person you just listened to.

Step Five
Listen to the recording.

Those who have done this exercise often report feeling healed by it. This might not happen the first or even second time through. Just keep doing the exercise until you feel heard.

Sometimes this is
a person's *first* experience
of truly feeling listened to and understood.

Two-handed recording, however effective, is not just a way to feel better. Each step is a powerful training in unconditional acceptance.

In **Step One**, we train to be present to our experience, to bring **conscious awareness** to what is. We learn to transcend the conditioned process of ignoring, avoiding, suppressing, rationalizing, denying, or intellectualizing our "reaction" to what is arising.

In **Step Two**, we learn **unconditional acceptance**. In listening without judgment, we open to the realization that we do encounter the entire range of human emotion, including anguish, rage, betrayal, disappointment, fear. There's nothing wrong with any of it, and with unconditional acceptance it isn't depressed.

In **Step Three**, we practice being **the wisdom, love and compassion** that can offer clear and practical comfort and assistance. This step may prove elusive but is essential. Most of us growing up received messages of judgment, rather than understanding. When we needed acceptance, we received and believed the message "there is something wrong with you." We learned to depress these "wrong" feelings. Only through the lens of compassion can we arrive at the truth of our inherent goodness.

In **Step Four**, we learn to **receive**

unconditional love. We make real for ourselves that who and how we are is *inherently* lovable and is unconditionally accepted and loved.

In **Step Five**, as we listen to the recording we just made, we realize that the love we offer and receive is the Unconditional Love that we are. In the words of Rumi:

You are gazing at the Light
With its own ageless eyes.

 Do Two-Handed Recording often, especially when you are feeling depressed.

More Encouragement

Here is a list of ways to work with depression. The next time you are depressed, do yourself a great kindness and pick one.

- Set a timer for 20 minutes and pay attention to your energy. Record what you noticed.
- Get up and move. Dance, go for a walk, do some yoga. What changed? R/L
- Throw a depression party. Make a recording about what you enjoyed most.
- Make a recording describing something you love.

This is training to redirect the attention. Repeat with what you're grateful for, what you appreciate in your life, what makes you laugh.
- Record "The List" on pages 88-89. Listen to the recording every morning for a week.

Meditation

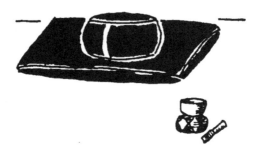

Meditation has been practiced throughout the world for thousands of years. In cultures where meditation has been an integral aspect of religious life, practitioners have learned that sitting in a certain posture — spine straight, body relaxed — is most conducive to being able to stay present. Physical pain and sleepiness are both minimized by sitting in this position.

A Meditation Posture

Sit on the first 1/3 of the cushion. If you are sitting on a bench, sit well forward. Adjust your leg position until you find one that can be maintained comfortably. Straighten your posture by pushing up from the base of the spine. Imagine that you are trying to touch the ceiling with the crown of your head. The chin will tuck slightly as you do this. The pelvis tilts slightly forward. The shoulders and abdomen relax. The eyes are open, slightly out of focus, and lowered, looking at the floor or wall at a 45-degree angle. The hands are in the cosmic mudra. The right hand is positioned a few inches below the navel, palm up. The left hand, also palm up, fits inside

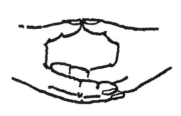 the right hand. The tips of the thumbs touch lightly, forming an oval.

The Breath

Focusing on the breath assists in staying present and alert in meditation. As you sit, breathe naturally and normally. On the first exhalation, count 1, on the next, count 2, and continue until you reach 10. At this point, start over at 1. Focus on the breath as it enters your body, fills your body, and leaves your body.

If attention wanders, gently bring it back to the present and begin counting again at 1.

Do this for up to 30 minutes. This is not a contest. The point is to be compassionately present and aware. Being gently present with yourself for 5 minutes will be much more helpful than beating yourself for 30. If your choice is between a kind of meditation or a long one, choose the kind one because the attitude of mind/heart is everything.

TALK WITH CHERI

Open Air
Open Air is Cheri's internet-based, call-in radio show.
Call in, listen, and download archived shows at
www.openairwithcherihuber.org.

Online Classes
Cheri conducts interactive online classes via email
on a wide variety of subjects
related to Zen Awareness Practice.
To be notified of future classes
sign up at www.livingcompassion.org.

Cheri's Practice Blog
Follow "Cheri Huber's Practice Blog"
at http://cherispracticeblog.blogspot.com

Books and Recordings
All Cheri Huber titles are available from your local
bookstore or online at www.keepitsimple.org.
Also available online are audio downloads and DVDs.

Visit www.livingcompassion.org to:

Sign up to receive notice of new email classes with Cheri Huber

Find a schedule of workshops and retreats

Find meditation groups in your area

Sign up for Reflective Listening Buddies

Sign up for Practice Everywhere

Sign up for a Zen Awareness Coach

Sign up for a Recording and Listening Trainer

Find out about our work in an impoverished community
in Zambia. Read blogs with updates from
the Africa Vulnerable Children Project.

Email: information@livingcompassion.org

Visit www.recordingandlistening.org
Read articles, access resources, challenge yourself
to fun exercises and get inspired!
You can even share your favorite
Recording and Listening insights and practices.

There Is Nothing Wrong with You
An Extraordinary Eight-Day Retreat
based on the book
There Is Nothing Wrong with You:
Going Beyond Self-Hate
by Cheri Huber

Inside each of us is a "persistent voice of discontent." It is constantly critical of life, the world, and almost everything we say and do. As children, in order to survive, we learned to listen to this voice and believe what it says.

This retreat is eight days of looking directly at how we are rejected and punished by the voices of self-hate and discovering how to let that go. Through a variety of exercises and periods of group processing, participants gain a clearer perspective on how they live their lives and on how to find compassion for themselves and others.

This work is challenging, joyous, fulfilling, scary, courageous, demanding, freeing, loving, kind, and compassionate —
compassionate toward yourself and everyone you will ever know.

For information on attending, contact:
Living Compassion/Zen Monastery Peace Center
P.O. Box 1756
Murphys, CA 95247
Email: information@livingcompassion.org
Website: www.livingcompassion.org

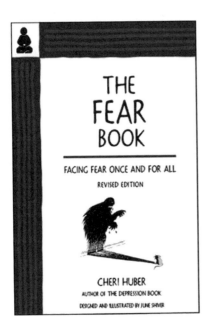

THE FEAR BOOK

FACING FEAR ONCE AND FOR ALL

REVISED EDITION

CHERI HUBER
AUTHOR OF THE DEPRESSION BOOK
DESIGNED AND ILLUSTRATED BY JUNE SHIVER

The Fear Book shows how to recognize fear as simple conditioned reactions to circumstances and how to mentor oneself into letting go of beliefs about "appropriate" responses to fear. The book includes a series of exercises for recognizing fear for what it is and overcoming its devastating effects.

ISBN: 9780991596324

THE Big BamBOOZLE

HOW YOU GET CONNED
OUT OF THE LIFE YOU WANT
AND WHAT TO DO ABOUT IT

CHERI HUBER & ASHWINI NARAYANAN
AUTHORS OF WHAT UNIVERSE ARE YOU CREATING?
DESIGNED & ILLUSTRATED BY JUNE SHIVER

Written in a humorous and lighthearted style, *The Big Bamboozle* illustrates through essays, stories, and examples what keeps us from choosing well-being, love, happiness, and joy as our life experience. The book contains a full year of practical exercises and nuggets of wisdom from those who have practiced with these teachings.

ISBN: 9780991596317